AF228563

US Flag

Julie Murray

Abdo Kids Junior
is an Imprint of Abdo Kids
abdobooks.com

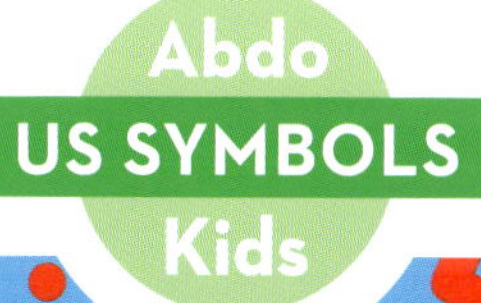

abdobooks.com

Published by Abdo Kids, a division of ABDO, P.O. Box 398166, Minneapolis, Minnesota 55439.
Copyright © 2020 by Abdo Consulting Group, Inc. International copyrights reserved in all countries.
No part of this book may be reproduced in any form without written permission from the publisher.
Abdo Kids Junior™ is a trademark and logo of Abdo Kids.

Printed in the United States of America, North Mankato, Minnesota.

052019

092019

THIS BOOK CONTAINS
RECYCLED MATERIALS

Photo Credits: Alamy, iStock, Shutterstock, ©Kevin Gill p.21/CC BY 2.0

Production Contributors: Teddy Borth, Jennie Forsberg, Grace Hansen

Design Contributors: Christina Doffing, Candice Keimig, Dorothy Toth

Library of Congress Control Number: 2018963329
Publisher's Cataloging-in-Publication Data

Names: Murray, Julie, author.

Title: US flag / by Julie Murray.

Description: Minneapolis, Minnesota : Abdo Kids, 2020 | Series: US symbols |
    Includes online resources and index.

Identifiers: ISBN 9781532185403 (lib. bdg.) | ISBN 9781532186387 (ebook) |
    ISBN 9781532186875 (Read-to-me ebook)

Subjects: LCSH: Flags--Juvenile literature. | United States--Flags--Juvenile
    literature. | Flags--United States--History--Juvenile literature. | Emblems,
    National--United States--Juvenile literature.

Classification: DDC 929.920973--dc23

Table of Contents

US Flag

The flag is a **symbol** of America.

RGIA BOUGAINVILLE TARAWA NEW BRITAIN 1944 MARSHALL ISLANDS MARIANAS ISLANDS PELELIU 1945 IWO JIMA OKINAWA ∗ KOREA 1950
REVOLUTIONARY WAR 1775–1783 ∗ FRENCH NAVAL WAR 1798–1801 ∗ TRIPOLI 1801–1805 ∗ WAR OF 1812–1815 ∗ FLORIDA INDIAN WA
UNCOMMON

The first flag was made
in 1777.

6

7

The flag is red, white,

and blue.

It has 13 red and white stripes. They stand for the first **13 colonies**.

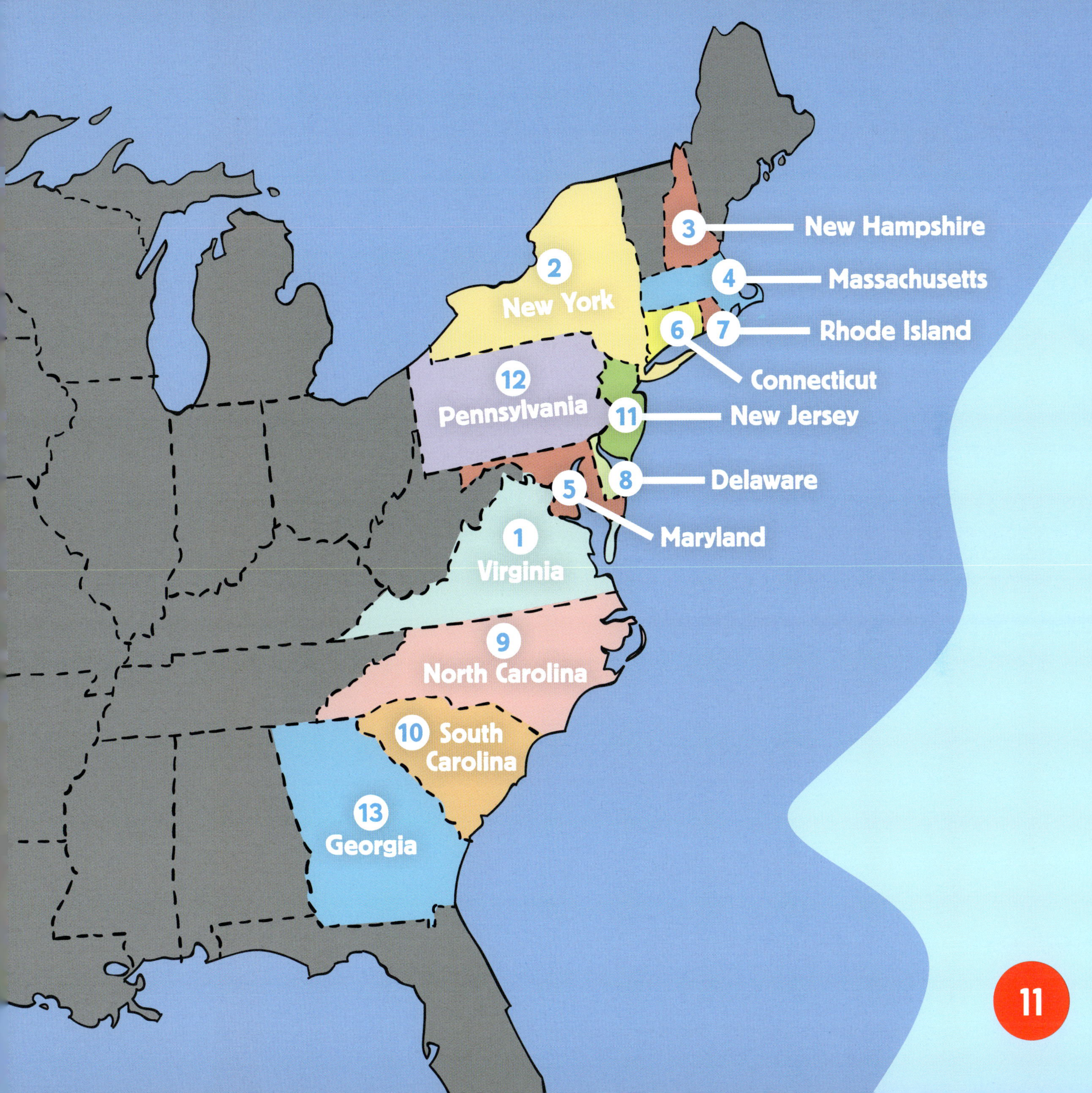

New Hampshire
Massachusetts
Rhode Island
Connecticut
New Jersey
Delaware
Maryland
3
4
6
7
11
8
5
2
New York
12
Pennsylvania
1
Virginia
9
North Carolina
10
South Carolina
13
Georgia
11

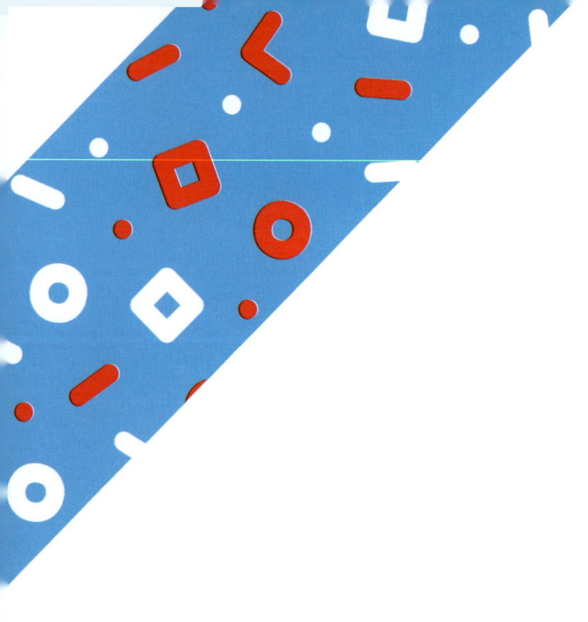

It has 50 stars. They stand

for the 50 states.

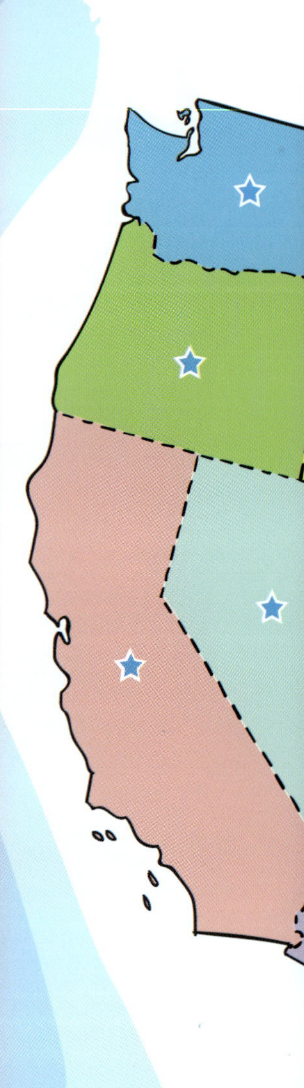

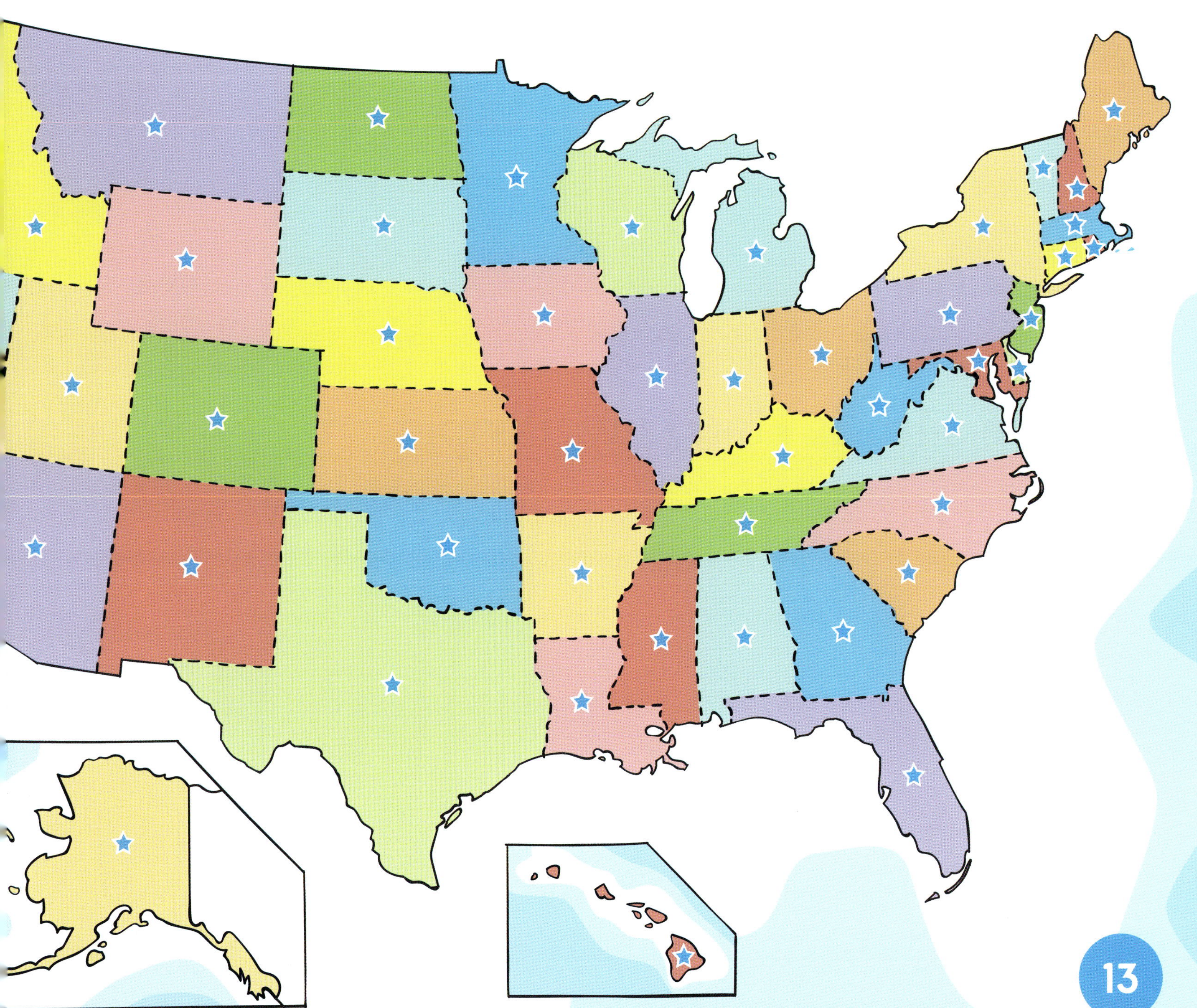

June 14th is Flag Day. People hang the flag on their homes.

Lil Bit
16

It is the 4th of July.

Jada waves the flag.

Kim marches in a **parade**.

She carries the flag.

EXCHANGE CLUB
JAYCEES
KIWANIS
WOMEN'S CLUB
LIONS
UNITED STATES POST OFFICE
pace
530

Look around. The flag is everywhere. It is even on the moon!

US Flag Throughout History

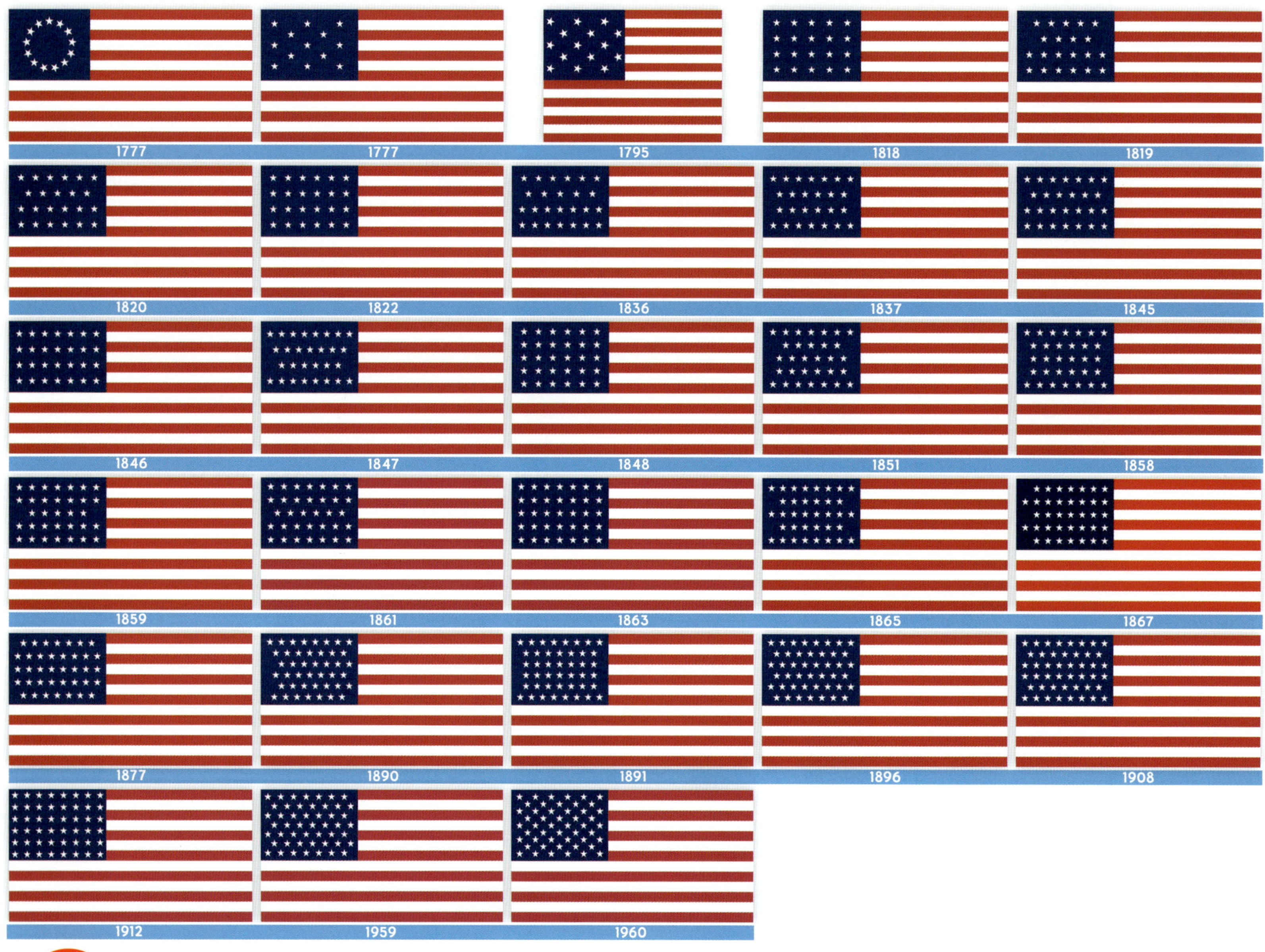

Glossary

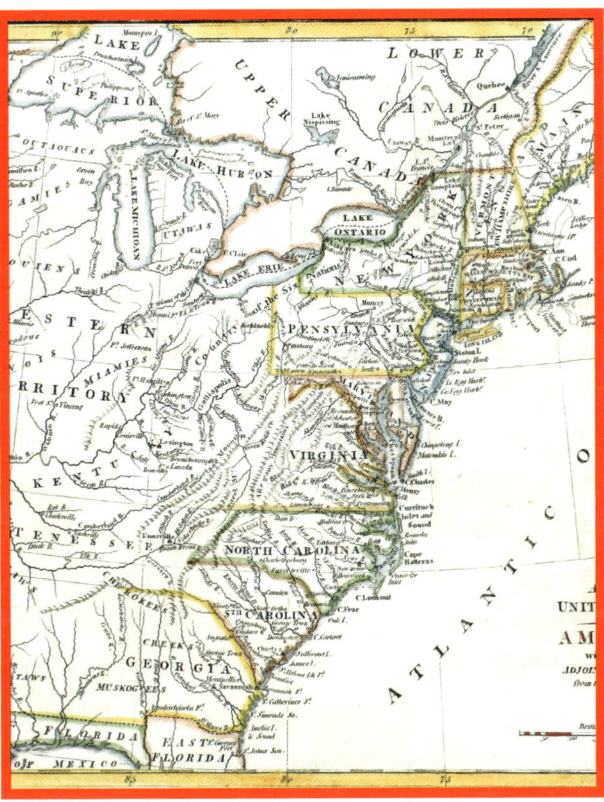

13 colonies

13 regions in America that were controlled by Great Britain until 1776. It was then that the colonies declared independence and formed the United States.

parade

a public procession of people, music, and more in front of a crowd as part of a celebration.

symbol

an object that represents something else.

Index

Visit **abdokids.com** to access crafts, games, videos, and more!

Use Abdo Kids code

UUK5403

or scan this QR code!